DISCOVER *your* INNER *Strength*

CUTTING EDGE GROWTH STRATEGIES
FROM THE INDUSTRY'S LEADING EXPERTS

To Andrea —
With ♥

INSIGHT PUBLISHING
SEVIERVILLE, TENNESSEE

Copyright © 2013
Published in the United States by

Insight Publishing Company
707 W. Main Street Suite 5
Sevierville, Tennessee 37862
www.insightpublishing.com

Disclaimer: This book is a compilation of ideas from numerous experts who have each contributed a chapter. As such, the views expressed in each chapter are of those who were interviewed and not necessarily of the interviewer or Insight Publishing.

ISBN-13 978-1-60013-017-5

TABLE OF CONTENTS

The interviews found in this book are conducted by
David E. Wright
President
Insight Publishing

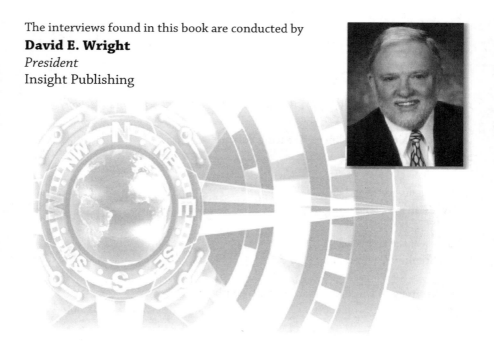

A Message from the Publisher

I've faced many challenges in my life and I know what it means to struggle. I sure wish I'd had this book during those times. We handpicked some of the most successful people we know who have had to learn how to discover their inner strength. The authors I interviewed for this book have the experience and knowledge that will help everyone learn a little more about this vital component for success— inner strength.

This book is custom designed for those who want to increase their skills and knowledge. Self-development is vital to success. One author made this poignant observation: "Self-development tends to fall to the bottom of the priority list for most people and they are not the only ones to suffer for this choice. Their family suffers. Their coworkers suffer. Their employees suffer. All of the crucial relationships in their life suffer because they are not being the absolute best they could truly be." If you strive for excellence and want valuable information about how some of the most successful people in business today have found their inner strength and achieved success, this book is the resource you need. People who want to hone their skills to cope with life's challenges will learn from what these authors have to say. I know that I did and I believe you will too. —David E. Wright

CHAPTER ONE
Practical Health and Wellness: Creating Balance

An Interview With...
Luanne Pennesi

David Wright (Wright)

Today we're talking with Luanne Pennesi. Luanne is a registered nurse practicing for over thirty years in both conventional and integrative medicine. She has dedicated her life to sharing information that motivates people to take back their personal power and lead happier, healthier, and more productive lives at any age. With a master's degree in Natural Health and a certification in Chinese medicine, including an extensive clinical and administrative background in adult medicine and oncology nursing, Luanne clearly has the experience and the credentials to help people reach their highest health potential. Her dynamic energy and humor makes understanding and actualizing new information easy.

Luanne, welcome to *Discover Your Inner Strength*.

Luanne Pennesi (Pennesi)

Thank you.

Wright

So will you give us some practical definitions of health and wellness?

Pennesi

Understanding the definition of health, I believe, is really paramount to becoming healthy, and there are so many angles from which you can define health. Politically, our systems define health as an absence of disease measured by illness, acuity, and an episode. Quite frankly, any illness that we have is the body's way of begging for our attention and saying, "Pay attention to me, there's something that you're doing that is not for my highest good." So unfortunately, our political definition of health, which governs our present healthcare system, might not be the most accurate definition. Philosophically, health is a value between opposite states of illness and wellness, ability and disability, or fitness and non-fitness, so it's like a dynamic somewhere in between.

Holistically, it's really about balance or harmony, of subtle energy fields in and around one's body and it encompasses the mind, the body, and the spirit, all interconnected.

Now, on a practical level, health really is all about the consequences of how we choose to live. It's about our choices—what we pick up and put in our mouth every day (our diet), if we exercise or not, and the use of things like recreational drugs or alcohol or cigarettes. It's how much happiness and joy we have every day—every thought you think affects every cell in your body and every cellular reaction in the body. It's also about how much fun you have; it's the kind of work you do, how much time you spend in relaxation or hobbies, or how you manage stress or not, and how much time you spend on improving yourself. All those things play into how healthy you are. So my definition of health is that it's an evolving consciousness about one's potential, not only physically but also mentally, emotionally, and spiritually. And a lot of it has to do with our belief systems. My work involves helping people to be optimally healthy on every single level.

Wright

Most people associate a good diet with health. How important is a healthy diet and what, in your opinion, does a healthy diet look like?

Pennesi

The diet is meant to fuel the body. Some people put better fuel in their cars than they do in their bodies. We've been conditioned to desire things that are sweet, salty, and crunchy. Many of us have been indoctrinated to eat to fill an emotional void or just to take away the feeling of hunger, when what we really need are some basic nutrients; and of course, we need water.

1. Water: One of the things I have noticed is that if people just got a little more hydrated with healthy fluids, they'd do great. Water alone is a wonderful detoxifier; it keeps the cells nice and healthy.
2. Complex carbohydrates: The carbohydrates that are healthy for you are complex carbohydrates like grains—amaranth, wild rice, brown rice, millet, etc.,—and squash, potatoes, and sprouted whole-grain breads.
3. Proteins: There are some healthy proteins that we can put into our bodies like beans, nuts, and seeds. One thing that most people don't realize is that seaweeds like dulse, kelp, arame, and hijiki are higher in protein than meat. It's amazing, and not only that, but there are also minerals that the body needs that alkalize the body, so seaweeds are a great protein to have. There are also other proteins, such as low mercury fish and soy proteins. Now, there has been some controversy about soy and I'll tell you that if you have a well-made, organic, non-genetically modified soy as a part of a balanced diet, it's really quite good for you. Be careful about soy if you have thyroid problems or allergies to it. We certainly don't want to have too much soy, but certainly, soy as part of a balanced diet is, in my professional opinion, healthy. Pumpkin seeds are high in zinc and it's very good for male hormone health. If you mix beans (think of all the different beans there are) and all the different grains, they create a complete protein. Then there are protein shakes made from powders out of rice protein, soy protein, whey protein, egg white protein, hemp protein, and even pea protein. Who knew that there were so many different sources of healthy protein shakes?
4. Healthy fats. It is very important to have healthy fats in our diet. One of the best fats we can put in the body are fish oils, coconut oil, nut and seed oils, and avocado oil. So this is not about having a low fat diet! Low fat diets are not healthy for the body. Our brain and many of our hormones and our nerves are all made of proteins and fats; they get their energy from carbohydrates. If people want to lose weight or they want to be as healthy as they can be, they need a good balance of protein, carbohydrates, and fats, but it doesn't end there.
5. Vitamins. I encourage people who live in industrialized societies to take vitamin supplements.
    a. One of the vitamins that we don't make is vitamin C. Humans, guinea pigs, and primates do not synthesize vitamin C, so we need take a

supplementation form of it. The question is how much? Well, if you knew how many different functions vitamin C played in the body, you'd take a lot of vitamin C—anywhere between 1,000 and 10,000 milligrams a day depending on your height, your weight, your activity, and what kind of environment you're living in. So vitamin C is wonderful.

b. Antioxidants, omega-3 fish oils, a good multivitamin, and Bcomplex are just some of the basic ones. There are many, many more that I discuss with people when I individualize protocols for them.

c. Then there are the minerals that you find in your green leafy vegetables and seaweeds or in supplements. We need to have lots and lots of those.

6. Green chlorophyll. People tend to not eat enough green chlorophyll. Green chlorophyll is what detoxifies our bodies naturally, so have a salad, or better yet make a green vegetable juice. Take vegetables like cucumbers and celery and parsley and then throw in some lemons and apples into a juicer. You will get a delicious, fresh green juice that cleanses all of the toxins out of the body. So if you're breathing in toxins, if you're exposed to electromagnetic pollution (we all are), and even if you're under a lot of stress, the green vegetable juices flush all that out through urine.

7. Red chlorophylls. The red chlorophylls are so very important for your body. Those are found in berries—strawberries, raspberries, blueberries, cherries, pomegranates, and cranberries. All of these red/orange/pink colored foods are very important, like the red skin of the apple. It's the red chlorophyll that heals our damaged cells. People who tend to look so well in their fifties, sixties, and seventies are usually the people who eat lots, and lots of red chlorophylls. You can get concentrated red chlorophyll pills and you can get red berry concentrates. Put the concentrates in a nice protein shake every day for your breakfast and you'll be loading your body up with all the phytonutrients that it needs.

8. Enzymes. You can get enzymes from papaya or pineapple, which are most important for biochemical reactions in the body. These are just some of the basics of a healthy diet.

Wright

So what else affects health?

Pennesi

Well, there are seven major areas I look at that really influence one's health:

1. Certainly your genetics—the genetics you get from each parent—play a role. But having a gene that may give you a propensity for a disease does not mean you will get the disease; it just means you need to put more attention into keeping yourself well fortified in regard to the "weaker" gene expression.

2. Peace of mind and bliss—knowing who you are, loving who you are, and living your life consistent with that. So many of us are living our lives adapting to other people's expectations of us. We lack self-discipline, we lose our playfulness, our ability to laugh out loud, and be spontaneous. These are the elements of what I call the spirit—peace of mind and bliss is really what our spirit is about. The practice of self-discipline is your capacity for unconditional love. Look into the eyes of a child, an animal— one of your pets—or a bird and you will see unconditional love. You know the look—they look at you as though you're just the greatest thing on the planet. That's part of your peace of mind and bliss, too. It's also your ability to laugh out loud and engage in activities and hobbies that make you lose track of time. It's a conscious choice of being happy and of course, most of all, it's your ability to express gratitude and appreciation.

3. The next area is managing your emotions. Many of us believe that when we have a negative emotion, we've got to hold onto it, stuff it into our bodies, and create a drama with it. But that is unnecessary. Negative emotions are there for us to get our attention; they are motivators for us to make change and if we see them as such—whether it's anxiety or fear or anger or depression or worry—they are there to get our attention. Negative emotions indicate that your spirit is broken; pay attention, something's not right. And it's usually something that we can't control. So when you're feeling an emotion, feel it; get into it, experience it, and then ask yourself what you need to mobilize—what do you need to do to learn from this event? You learn and you take your lesson. You can leave the negative emotions behind and march forward with your new lesson. It's a wonderful way of living of your life without holding on to that emotion and carrying grudges and holding on to old pain from the past. When you have permission to let these things go, your whole physiology changes. Part of that is having nurturing, healthy relationships in your life on every different level.

4. The next area is managing your physiology, which has to do with your diet, taking supplements, exercising your body daily, including having

a healthy sex life. It's also about the quality of your breathing and how well you are eliminating (moving your bowels). We ingest food and liquid into our bodies and these substances are processed. Remember, we've got twenty-eight feet of intestines and three to four more feet of large intestines in addition to the small intestines, so we need to make sure that we're moving our waste out on a regular basis. So making sure that you're moving your bowels every day, at least once a day is important. How about posture and alignment? Chiropractic adjustments help to make sure that our spines are aligned. Walking and sitting using good posture is imperative because when the spine is out of line (remember, the spine is your lifeline!) it feeds every organ in your body and every muscle. When the spine is aligned, our body functions much more efficiently.

5. Here's another area: rest and sleep. So many of us aren't getting enough sleep! We're living such busy lives that we lack the proper sleep. When we're sleeping, that's when our body is detoxifying—it's like recharging your battery. So we need to have a good solid sleep, anywhere from six to eight hours.

   As we age we also have to keep our hormones in balance, and there are many ways to do it naturally. We don't have to use synthetic drugs. One of the most important things I've learned since I've studied holistic medicine is that there is a plant out there on the planet that can rebalance any imbalance in the human body, whether it's a mental imbalance or physiological imbalance. When you understand that and you open yourself to the information, you'll see that plants don't have the side effects that many of our drugs have, when used correctly. I always start with a natural approach, then, if people need synthetic drugs to help them with an imbalance, by all means we'll work with a physician and bring it right into their protocol. There are two more areas that affect your health.

6. One is your physical environment—the climate of your home, your workplace, your car, or public transportation; personal hygiene, environmental hygiene, and attacks by microbes in your environment. Then a very important piece that is the root of many of our chronic illnesses is heavy metal toxicity that we get from the strangest places, like silver fillings in teeth and aluminum in deodorants and aluminum pots and pans, just to name a few.

7. The last thing that affects our health is our energy—the fields of energy in and around us. We have to look at our internal energy and

the energy around us, receiving the intentions of other people, and cleaning ourselves on the cellular level. That includes releasing old pain and being able to ground your energy every day.

So a lot of things are in play when you look at what influences your health.

Wright

There's been a lot of research on the affect that exercise has on long-term health. How important is it and what's the best type?

Pennesi

Exercise is so very important. We have hundreds of muscles and we need to use them. I encourage people to find an exercise that works for them. Not everyone likes to go to a gym, so some people work out on their own. Other people like being with groups, some people like sports, and other people enjoy a nice long walk or a hike, so I encourage an exercise that works for each person. There are people who say, "Well, I'm sitting at a computer all day, I don't have the time to exercise." Well yeah, you do. You can do exercises sitting right in the chair. There are things you can do sitting right in your chair at work. You can put your right elbow to your left knee and then switch your left elbow to your right knee and just sit there. Then just do opposition crunches and you'll have a beautiful waistline. You can do seated squats, what I call "butt cheek squeezes," waist bends . . there are so many things that you can do while sitting. So why exercise? Well number one it increases the oxygenation of your body, and oxygen increases your energy. Virus, parasites, yeast, cancers, and anaerobic bacteria cannot grow where there is a lot of oxygen. So we encourage people to do a lot of breath work while they're doing their exercises. And just as a little side bar, your green vegetable juices also provide loads of oxygen for your body.

The other thing that exercise does is it increases your metabolism, so it helps you burn fat. In addition, you end up with more endurance, you have more strength, and even better than that, when you're exercising and moving your circulation, you're removing toxins from all of your organs, especially your liver, and lymphatic system. It also helps your colon with elimination, it benefits the lungs, the skin, and the bladder, that's why sweating is so great for you.

Also, when you exercise, you increase your endorphin levels and you balance serotonin levels. Those are the elements that help you maintain a happy mood. So when people work out regularly they seem to be in better moods; best of all, they like the way they look. In Chinese medicine practitioners understand that the tone of the skeletal muscle is a reflection of the efficiency of your digestion. So the more toned your muscles are, the more efficient your digestion is. That's a great motivation right there, if you have any issues with your digestion.

Exercising is a manifestation of focus, attention, and discipline. Those are the three hallmarks of functioning from a higher, more self-actualized place. So yes, exercise is very, very important. Do what works for you. Always stretch before and after to prevent injury and to stabilize the body. I encourage people to do something cardiovascular or aerobic like stationary bike-riding, dancing, swimming, and so on,\ and then combine that with some kind of resistance workout like circuit training or free weights or calisthenics. A fun thing to do is to get a little rebounder and do some bouncing! Bouncing is far and away one of the best exercises you can do. So combine them, figure out what works out best for you and work out five to six days a week.

Wright

So what is the role of genetics, or your constitution on your health?

Pennesi

Well, I think genetics has received a lot of attention in terms of how it influences our health. The term "constitution" is used to describe the physical, emotional, and mental inheritance that we receive from our parents. In one sense, it's our genetic makeup, which is determined at the moment of conception. Traditional Chinese Medicine teaches that the energy from both parents is stored in the child's kidneys because that's where the life energy sits—it's our life force and is responsible for our growth, development, and reproduction. It also determines our lifespan. So even though we all have the same biological template, our propensities from each parent are expressed differently with each conception. Determinate factors in your genetics include health issues such as if either of your parents used cigarettes or recreational drugs, if either of them had a medical problem(s), their nutritional status, if they have weak constitutions, the quality of their sleep/rest cycles. In other words, their state of health at the time of your conception affects your health at birth. So clearly the healthier both parents are, the healthier the child will be. Also, remember that we each have innate strengths and weaknesses. For instance, I had the same exact diet and lifestyle as my siblings, and yet each of us grew up very differently in terms of our propensities for illness. I had severe acne and my siblings did not. So you really appreciate this when you see that there are certain differences and yet there are other areas in which we are all the same. Again, it comes from your genetics.

While it's important to understand, it doesn't dictate whether you're going to be healthy or not, and one of the things that I oppose is if a woman is told that she has some kind of genetic propensity for breast cancer, she is told to have bilateral mastectomies. In my opinion as a licensed health professional, I would encourage her to examine her lifestyle and fortify her immune system before having cancer-free breasts removed preventively. Just because you have a gene that may form a propensity for illness, it doesn't necessarily mean that you're going to get the illness.

What it does give you, though, is a heads up that you have to overcompensate for the weaker areas in your genetics, and that's a big part of my work with people. It's so exciting to see that when people use these tools, oh my goodness, their health just skyrockets.

Wright

So what other aspects of our biology are important for optimal health?

Pennesi

Well, let's take a look. We talked about nutrition and I mentioned juicing, and supplements. As I said, these are very, very important.

One of the most important things we need to do is to detoxify. We have to look at what in our life is adding toxins to our body. It could be our emotions, our environment; it could be smoking cigarettes or regular use of alcohol or caffeine. Caffeine is not a healthy substance to ingest at all. Caffeine affects our physiology amazingly. It depletes and dehydrates you and it removes many of your vitamins, especially your B vitamins and folic acid, which are so important. So I encourage use of substitutes for caffeine.

We also need to eliminate dairy products. We don't look like cows, we don't have the same physiology as they do, and we don't have their immune system, so when we put dairy products in our body, we create phlegm throughout the body; we become Petri dishes for infections. There are many dairy alternatives. Coconut milk is one of my favorites, then there is rice milk, soy milk, nut milks (like almond milk) and all of those are great.

Sugar and artificial sweeteners are far and away the worst things we can put inour bodies. There are healthy sugars like stevia and agave nectar, and xylitol. These are natural sugars that are far better for the body that don't increase blood sugar. Carbonated drinks like sodas and seltzer are injected

9

with gases that wear away our bones. I see many men now even getting osteoporosis when they don't have to; they just need to let go of all that soda.

Even whole wheat is not healthy for us. As a society, we've grown to become allergic to whole wheat flour. But there are many other alternatives, like spelt, and sprouted whole grain products. Before the grain actually blooms, you've got the sprout where concentrated energy and concentrated nutrition are. So sprouted whole grain bread is the best choice. Also available is sprouted whole grain pasta. So there are many alternatives to whole wheat flour. I also encourage people to eat organic produce as much as possible, mostly because they're grown in mineral rich soil and there are no pesticides on them. Depleted soil, pesticides, rodenticides, and herbicides get into our bodies through non-organic produce and wreak havoc on our cells. So healthy produce like organic potatoes, squash, sweet potatoes, yams, fruits and vegetables, and beans and grains is an essential part of a diet that is healthy for us. When you start eating healthy, your body is going to eliminate better, it's going to detoxify better, and age very slowly. Then we have to repair the damage done to the cells, and that's of course what those red fruit phytonutrients, your healthy essential fatty acids, and healthy proteins do. And of course, we also need to include emotional repair. You've got to learn to forgive people. Forgiving is far and away one of the best things we do for our bodies because it stops the production of internal stress hormones that we hold onto subconsciously.

Finally, there's rejuvenation, and that's when you challenge your body on every level. I went from just exercising so that I didn't gain weight to exercising to really tone and trim my body. Finally, I moved on to becoming a world class athlete. I went into rejuvenation by challenging my body, and now I can see what my body is capable of doing. I never imagined that I could be this fit at my age. As we age, we think that we've got to slow down, but I don't agree with that at all. I've done the New York City Marathon with seventy-, eighty-, and ninety-year-olds, and if they can do it, you know, what's my excuse? So those are some of the things that affect the body.

Wright

So what is the role of self-esteem in regard to our health?

Pennesi

Self-esteem is everything. I can give people all the information they want, and they can manipulate their physiology with vitamins, but, if they have low self-esteem they're not going to have the incentive—that passion, that drive—to be self-discipline and to do whatever it takes to get themselves to live at their highest level.

As a holistic nurse, I would say that most often, the cause of many diseases is low self-esteem. So when I work with people, I often start with just building their self-esteem up. I familiarize them with those six pillars that Nathaniel Branden speaks of:

1. The first one is living consciously, understanding that events happen; life happens. Two things happen when there is a life event: you can either be a victim of your life circumstances or you can build your character from them. There is a choice. Most of us don't think there's a choice. And in life, pain is inevitable but suffering is an option. We are a society that's built on the drama of suffering. But suffering is dumb. If you're in pain, that's your body's way of telling you to pay attention and help. So if you pay attention and help, you'll see that the pain usually goes away. Keep your self-esteem strong by understanding that in life there is really no stress; there are two things: there is good information to which you need to respond, and the rest is free live entertainment.

2. The second principle is the practice of self-acceptance. I ask people to look at their thoughts, actions, and emotions without self-repudiation. Experience them without having to slash away at yourself because it doesn't meet someone's expectations of you. Love you for who you are and what you've got. Every single one of us is unique. We all have greatness and we all have something to contribute to make this planet better because we were here.

3. The next one is the practice of self-responsibility. Understand that you're the author of your choices and actions and that no one is coming to save you. You've got to direct your own life.

4. Next is the practice of self-assertiveness. This, in my opinion, is about just being authentically you, not hiding your feelings, and not worrying if people disapprove of you. It's being respectful of people around you without needing them to accept you. When you suppress or deny your feelings it's usually out of fear, and that's when self-esteem goes right down.

5. Then I encourage people to live purposely. In other words, do whatever you need to do to get whatever you want. Each of us deserves that.

6. And finally, practice personal integrity. Be real, be truthful, and keep your promises.

Wright

So how significant is management of our physical environment on our health?

Pennesi

Well, our physical environment plays a huge role, so I encourage people to look at the basics. Number one, look at the air you're breathing. You can purchase little mini air purifiers that you can hang around your neck. I have an air purifier that plugs into the cigarette lighter of my car, too. These things are wonderful to help you only breathe in healthy air. Then there are larger units you can put into your home. When you have clean, pure, healthy air, you're protecting your lungs from damage.

Next, look at water. Most of our water, whether it's from a well or it's municipal water, has some kind of treatment done to it. So I encourage people to get good water filtration units for their homes. You can get one for the whole house or you can get something for the kitchen and then something for your shower. Make sure you have good clean water coming into your home.

Then examine the chemicals in your home. There are natural, planet friendly products for cleaning. You can use something as simple as peroxide. Take a little brown bottle of peroxide, put a spritzer top on it, and spray your shower curtain or shower door, tiles, and fixtures. It kills everything, and you don't even have to wipe it away. Same thing is true with rubbing alcohol. Put a spritzer top on a bottle of rubbing alcohol, spray your surfaces, and wipe it off (alcohol requires friction).

The other thing to use is very, very, very diluted bleach to clean floors (1:10), and vinegar for mirrors and glass. These are very inexpensive. There are even laundry magnets and papaya bleach so you don't have spend money on laundry detergents.

There are so many wonderful things to bring into your home—there's a whole other world out there when you learn about natural approaches to living.

I encourage people to get rid of wall-to-wall carpets, and consider the materials of the pillow you're sleeping on. Look at how much time we spend on our pillows.

Make sure you have a good hypoallergenic cover for it.

There is full spectrum lighting that is much better than regular lighting. One of the greatest things we can do in our environment is to get rid of microwave ovens. They are so dangerous. They denature the food and fluids; and remember, the whole purpose of putting food in our body is to put energy into it. When you put any food in a microwave oven, even if you're heating up water, it denatures it, taking the energy right out of it. Not only that but the microwaves are very harmful to human cells, so stay away from microwaves altogether—get rid of them. Toaster ovens, stovetops, and convections ovens are all fine to use.

Make sure no one wears shoes inside your home. Think of it, it's just reasonable. Look at all the microbes and parasites, the garbage out there and the dirt that is coming from the outside into your home when people wear shoes inside your home.I encourage people to have people take their shoes off. You can get those little thin shoe covers that people can wear instead. This practice keeps your house clean, keeps the microbe population down, and prevents infections. Remember, infections are one of the top sources of chronic illness in our population.

Even our cell phones are dangerous. You have to make sure that you have a cell phone shield where the sound comes out of your cell phone. This is especially applicable to your cordless phones as well because you want to protect your brain from all that electromagnetic toxicity. I've been seeing more and more young people with acoustic neuromas. Neuromas are the tumors that form right beyond the ear from chronic electromagnetic and radiation exposure from cell phones.

And of course, everyone should have a carbon monoxide detector in the house as well as smoke detectors.

Always reuse bags when you go to the grocery store, use cloth bags so that we're not polluting the planet with all kinds of plastic. There is even natural pest control.

Make sure, before you eat all your fruits and vegetables, that you're cleaning them off thoroughly. There are commercial veggie washes available.

I think one of the most important things people can do is to declutter their physical environment. Go through all of your "stuff" and give it away, sell it, or throw it away—use it or get rid of it. We need to understand that our physical environment is a reflection of what's going on in our head and what's going on our bodies. This is similar to the art of Feng shui. So when you have a lot of clutter and junk and stuff that you're holding onto, it usually means you're holding on to junk and clutter in your emotions and junk and clutter in your body. Remember how good it felt when you collected a bag full of old clothes and gave it away? You just feel lighter, and you travel farther with a lighter load. So I encourage people to really, really declutter their physical environment and keep it clean using all natural products.

Wright

So what about day-to-day rituals concerning personal hygiene?

Pennesi

I encourage people to start out with natural shampoos, cosmetics, and bath and shower products—things that are planet friendly and much safer to put on our bodies. Remember, your skin is a semi-permeable membrane, so it absorbs the things that we put on it. Consider using natural face washes and avoid cake soaps because they harbor bacteria. The pump dispensers are a better choice. In terms of oral care, I encourage people to use toothpastes that are made with peroxide, baking soda, sea salt, or natural toothpaste, without fluoride or saccharin.

There has never ever been a scientific study that proved that fluoride has any effect on the development of cavities. In fact, it's toxic to the body. I discourage any child from having fluoride treatments on their teeth. If they're eating a healthy diet and they're maintaining good oral hygiene, there is no need for them to have fluoride in their mouth.

Another thing that I really discourage people from getting is silver or mercury fillings. It is one of the chief causes of heavy metal toxicity in our society today. There has also never ever been any proof that showed that mercury fillings were safe; they're not.

I remember when I was a nurse in the hospital; if our blood pressure machine fell over and the mercury fell out, you had to go through a whole ritual with special gloves to handle the toxic mercury. And that's the mercury that is going into tooth fillings! It's a contradiction. I discourage people from having silver fillings placed in their mouths. There are beautiful biocompatible composites that holistic dentists can put in now. I also encourage people to soak their toothbrushes in peroxide at least three times a week to disinfect them. Store your toothbrush and cups inside of a cabinet. Most of us keep our toothbrushes in the vicinity of toilet bowl. When the toilet is flushed and the lid is left up, microbes from the toilet will now settle on the toothbrush.

These little things make such a big difference. There are also natural deodorants that use baking soda. They are made with Thai crystals and enzyme deodorants that are far better for the body than the standard deodorants with aluminum in them. Remember, it's aluminum that's causing a lot of the symptoms of diseases like Alzheimer's.

Heavy metal toxicity is a huge factor in disease today.

Wright

Many of us are in high stress jobs and then we're running home and raising our children. What are some of the ways to manage stress?

Pennesi

The first thing I would encourage people to do is take time out every single day to relax and reflect, or better yet, to meditate. And there is no right time of day to do it. Now, when most of us think of meditation we think of someone dressed in a toga closing their eyes going, "ohmm . . ." Well, it doesn't necessarily have to be that way. I encourage people to use their senses when they're meditating—have something that you can see, have something that you can listen to, whether it's through a headset or on a music system, but have sound or have something that you can watch.

Take time out every day and sit for at least a half an hour and learn to ground your energy. Most people have wonderful energy but they just don't know how to manage it. We try so hard to manage all the important things in our life. Yet there are things out there that you just can't control, and when you can't control something or someone, that's what we call "stress." Stress is actually the frustration we feel when we are trying to control an uncontrollable situation. So when you pull back and you ground your energy, you're able to use your intuition to problem-solve better and to manage the conflict more effectively.

Here are some great ways to meditate: First of all, know that there is no outcome to meditation, the only outcome really is a deep sense of relaxation and bliss. Meditation strengthens the breath. And again, you're increasing oxygenation of the body. In Chinese Medicine, the lungs rule the part of the immune system that wards off externally induced infections, so when you have a strong breath—a strong lung energy—you tend to not pick up microbes in your environment. Plus it grounds your energy, so it helps you sleep better. I encourage people to do their meditation before they go to bed if they have trouble sleeping. And it can be as simple as taking a hot bath with a couple of cups of Epsom salts, a bottle of peroxide, and maybe a couple drops of lavender oil. Put some beautiful music on and just lie back and relax. So many people don't give themselves permission to feel that kind of relaxation. We've been conditioned to feel that if we are not busy doing something that we are not worthy. Well, let me tell you, only the people who take really good care of themselves first will be better able to be more helpful to other people. So this is one of the hallmarks of health— learning to sit down and ground your energy.

There are progressive relaxation tapes out there. There are yoga, or Tai Chi, or Chi-Gong classes. Just getting a therapeutic facial sometimes is wonderful. You can get a healing touch treatment like Reiki or Hands on

Healing treatments from healing touch practitioners. There are affirmation tapes by wonderful people like Louise Hay and Alan Cohen.

When you listen to positive statements that apply to you and you replace the junk in your head with positive statements, you will see that your life indeed changes for the better. Remember that 99 percent of your life is in your head so if you take out the junk—just like you declutter your physical environment and keep moving your bowels—and you put the good stuff in your head/body/environment, it changes your life!

There are other things like guided meditation tapes, alpha induction tapes, and alpha waves. Alpha sounds are the ones that relax you as though you're listening to a harp or some other soothing sound.

Then there are group meditations. Sometimes you can sit in nature or enjoy special time with your pets or do some gardening. People love to garden because it's so relaxing. There's also guided imagery and visualization. You can get these tools right out of the library.

Then there are flotation tanks. These induce controlled sensory deprivation. Try this if you're really ready to do some advanced meditation. Sometimes having a good message is wonderful. Then there are meditation videos.

I have something that I plug in to my computer called "Sacred Geometry." It's a special CD-ROM that you put on your computer, so for those of you who have to sit at computers all day, here is a way to meditate at work! The colors and the graphics are magnificent, as is the sound. You can just sit there and meditate right at your desk.

Creative minds always find a way to make things work for themselves and these are just some suggestions to help you ground your energy and deal with stress.

Wright

So what are the root causes of chronic illnesses and premature aging?

Pennesi

There is not only one thing that accelerates your aging and creates chronic illness, but there are certainly specific things that we can consider. Number one is chronic inflammation. So many of us are allergic—we've had delayed reaction allergies to foods or to things in our environment. Chronic allergens and environmental toxins add to illness.

If you're taking public transportation every day or if you're in an automobile every day, you're breathing in exhaust and toxins. We have so much air pollution on our planet; hopefully we're at a time now where we're going to turn that around. There are chronic toxins that come into the body that create inflammation.

Over time, the inflammation confuses your immune system and you become prone to what we call autoimmune illnesses. Those are illnesses like fibromyalgia, multiple sclerosis, Alzheimer's, diabetes, Parkinson's disease, cardiovascular disease, and arthritis. So when you're eating foods that are full of toxins and you're breathing in air that's full of toxins, when you're getting electromagnetic toxicity, and you're holding on to negative emotions and stressing out over things unnecessarily, all these things create inflammation in the body. That alone can certainly add to aging you prematurely and creating autoimmune illnesses.

The other element affecting our health is chronic infections. This includes viruses (e.g., herpes, hepatitis, and chronic fatigue syndrome), bacteria (e.g., pneumonia, urinary tract infections, cellulitis), Lyme's disease (caused by a spirochete), and yeast infections.

If we get an infection, we're given antibiotics and the physician doesn't suggest that you take probiotics. Probiotics are the healthy bacteria that are killed in our bowels when we take antibiotics, which then causes diarrhea. There are natural antibiotics to use like garlic, oil of oregano, and grapefruit seed extract. There are number of them that are very, very good for the body that don't have the terrible side effects that our synthetic drugs have—killing off our healthy bacteria in the bowel. Chronic infections really drain the body and they accelerate the aging process as well. Life events also create inflammation in the body. Death, loss of a job, loss of a pet, ending relationships, weather disasters, accidents, and the like are perfect examples.

Life events sometimes can really take their toll on us, so that's why it's so important to see your life events as opportunities to build your character and then pull back and make sure you spend the time to take good care of yourself after you've experienced it.

We need to also consider the affect of hormone imbalances. For example, we need to make sure that we don't have high sugar diets because then our internal insulin pump ends up turning on us and we develop insulin resistance, which leads to hypoglycemia and diabetes.

People who aren't sleeping well enough at night don't make enough melatonin. Keeping the room dark and supplementing with melatonin can be very helpful. Also, as we age our sex hormones decline. Thankfully, there are "bio-identical hormones" that are made by taking plant hormones (plants have estrogen and progesterone just as we do) and we bio-electrically turn them into human hormones!

They're very natural, they don't cause cancer, and they help you to maintain a healthy body even as you're aging. So hormone balance is a very, very important. And of course, as I mentioned before, heavy metal toxicity is a huge contributor to poor health and chronic illness. There are so many things in our environment and in our diets that add heavy metals to the body. You really want to make sure that you get them out of your body. Green vegetable juices help to take those out rapidly, as does healthy algae, like chlorella and spirulina. So when you're eating consciously and you're staying away from these things in your environment, it really makes a huge, huge difference.

As we age, the body takes calcium from our bones and deposits it in our organs. Over time, the organs get more and more rigid, therefore they work less efficiently, and eventually we're supposed to die in our sleep. But that doesn't have to happen if you have healthy hormones in the body, you're exercising, and you're giving your body what it needs to work for you. We could live up to one hundred and fifty or one hundred and sixty if we would only give our body what it needs to work for us!

Wright

How effective is having healthy, supported relationships to our health versus having strained, unsupportive ones?

Pennesi

I ask people to make a list of the supportive people in their life and then the dysfunctional people. Usually the dysfunctional list is pretty long. Healthy relationships are just so very important. Louise Hay said it so well, "All relationships are important because they reflect how you feel about yourself. If you are constantly beating yourself up thinking that everything that goes wrong is your fault, or that you are always a victim, then you are going to attract the type of relationship that reinforces those beliefs in you." I ask people to take a good hard look at the kinds of people they have in their life. She goes on to say, "Likewise, if you believe that a higher power has surrounded you with truly loving people . . . then those are the types of relationships you will ultimately draw to yourself." You need healthy relationships in your life if you're going to be healthy for sure.

One of the things we need to realize is that there are no perfect matches for us—people are not going to be in our lives to fill in our gaps. The healthiest relationships are those where each person perceives himself or herself as great, whole, and complete and when their energies merge together they are both even more of who they imagined they could be because each is in the other's life. That's a healthy relationship. It is based on mutual respect, admiration, and candor.

Most people lose their whole identities to their relationships. And not only their relationships with their partners, but also with their kids. Sometimes we lose our identity to our jobs. I encourage people to maintain their own identity and maintain their jobs and their relationships as an extension of who they are—to help them to be more of who they are and vice versa.

There are actually six things that I encourage people to do in order to really keep their relationships strong. I learned these from one of my most respected mentors (and coauthor of this book!), Brian Tracy. One of the first things is to be agreeable.

People feel valuable and important when you come from a place of love. So there's a difference between criticizing someone and offering constructive counsel. Sometimes it's just the words you use. Instead of saying things like, "You know what's wrong with you," you could try saying something like, "Have you ever considered—" and offer your suggestion.

The next thing is to be accepting. We're so busy trying to make everybody be like us, but that will never happen because there is no one just like each one of us. So accept people for who they are. Sometimes just a smile is just enough.

The next is appreciation—always have gratitude. Even if you're in a marriage, make sure you're still saying please and thank you and being courteous to the other person. Appreciation is so very important. We all want approval, and one of the great motivators is being approved of by other people. Praiseworthiness is one of the best measures of high self-esteem. Praise people when it's deserved and be very specific.

The other thing is admiration. Compliment people sincerely. When you find the good in people, they're going to find the good in you.

Then of course, the most amazing thing that keeps relationships strong is attention; this is what life is—the study of attention. It reflects interest, and you feel that a person is important if you're giving him or her your undivided attention.

Another thing I encourage people to consider is that we all come into this life with different life energies. I got this information from health and nutrition expert, Gary Null, and it has had an amazing affect on my life. There are three different types of energies:

1. *Dynamic energies:* People who have dynamic energy are very charismatic. They love to create change and they love getting out there and making big changes. They always see the big picture and are born leaders.

2. *Adaptives:* Adaptives are not charismatic and they don't like change. You give them a set of rules to live by and they will adapt to it. They are the hard workers of society—the glue that makes the community successful.

3. *Creatives:* Creatives are actors and musicians, muses and artists. They are people who dedicate their lives to art. They're a different breed of people who tend to work best with each other versus the other life energies.

So many of us are trying to make other people our energy. For example, if I'm a dynamic energy and you're a creative energy it's a waste of time to have me to expect you to become a dynamic energy so I can have a better relationship with you. There are some relationships that are better left alone. With this understanding, you can enjoy relationships on different levels. I have friends who are very, very creative but I couldn't imagine living in a house with them because I couldn't imagine living the way a creative person lives. It's just their way of connecting to their worlds. But it doesn't mean I can't enjoy a wonderful relationship with them.

So I encourage people to look at the relationships in their lives and see which ones are there to help them with their self-esteem or to appreciate something that they're not or to discern if there is someone they have lost their identity to. The greatest gift you can give yourself is permission to let go of toxic relationships with love. If people are constantly putting you down to make themselves feel good, these are not healthy relationships. Look for someone who shares your same temperament and has the same values and the same life energy so that you can live more in harmony. And have other relationships that compliment what you're doing so that your relationships are nurturing instead of destructive and condescending.

Wright

Well, what a great conversation. I really have learned a lot today. I'm going to have to take this back and study it. You've covered so much information; I'm sure that our readers are really going to be glad to read this chapter.

Pennesi

I encourage people to be self-informed and not indoctrinated. It's only through reason that the truth is revealed and the information I've shared is all based in universal truth; it applies to everyone.

Wright

Today we've been talking with Luanne Pennesi, a registered nurse. She has dedicated her life to sharing information, as she has done today, that motivates people to take back their personal power and lead happier, healthier, and more productive lives—as she states—at any age.

Luanne, thank you so much for being with us today on *Discover Your Inner Strength*.

Pennesi

It is an absolute pleasure to be here.

Luanne Pennesi, a registered nurse practicing for over 30 years in both conventional and integrative medicine, shares information that motivates people to take back their personal power and lead happier more productive lives at ANY age.

Her work is the missing link between the confusing, overwhelming and conflicting information about "new age" or "alternative" approaches to health and anti-aging and the practical application of real-time, commonsense, scientifically based information to help you take full control over your health and longevity and often save your own life naturally. She makes learning fun as she presents wholistic health concepts in a manner that is easy to understand and to integrate.

Luanne Pennesi, RN, MS
Professional speaker, trainer, and consultant
973.766.2214
www.metropolitanwellness.com
whnn@aol.com

CHAPTER TWO
Attitude is Everything

An Interview With...
Dr. Kenneth Blanchard

David Wright (Wright)

Few people have created a positive impact on the day-to-day management of people and companies more than Dr. Kenneth Blanchard. He is known around the world simply as Ken, a prominent, gregarious, sought-after author, speaker, and business consultant. Ken is universally characterized by friends, colleagues, and clients as one of the most insightful, powerful, and compassionate men in business today. Ken's impact as a writer is far-reaching. His phenomenal best-selling book, *The One Minute Manager*®, coauthored with Spencer Johnson, has sold more than thirteen million copies worldwide and has been translated into more than twenty-five languages. Ken is Chairman and "Chief Spiritual Officer" of the Ken Blanchard Companies. The organization's focus is to energize organizations around the world with customized training in bottom-line business strategies based on the simple, yet powerful principles inspired by Ken's best-selling books.

Dr. Blanchard, welcome to *Discover Your Inner Strength*.

Dr. Ken Blanchard (Blanchard)

Well, it's nice to talk with you, David. It's good to be here.

David Wright (Wright)

I must tell you that preparing for your interview took quite a bit more time than usual. The scope of your life's work and your business, the Ken Blanchard Companies, would make for a dozen fascinating interviews.

Before we dive into the specifics of some of your projects and strategies, will you give our readers a brief synopsis of your life—how you came to be the Ken Blanchard we all know and respect?

Blanchard

Well, I'll tell you, David, I think life is what you do when you are planning on doing something else. I think that was John Lennon's line. I never intended to do what I have been doing. In fact, all my professors in college told me that I couldn't write. I wanted to do college work, which I did, and they said, "You had better be an administrator." So I decided I was going to be a Dean of Students. I got provisionally accepted into my master's degree program and then provisionally accepted at Cornell because I never could take any of those standardized tests.

I took the college boards four times and finally got 502 in English. I don't have a test-taking mind. I ended up in a university in Athens, Ohio, in 1966 as an Administrative Assistant to the Dean of the Business School. When I got there he said, "Ken, I want you to teach a course. I want all my deans to teach." I had never thought about teaching because they said I couldn't write, and teachers had to publish. He put me in the manager's department.

I've taken enough bad courses in my day and I wasn't going to teach one. I really prepared and had a wonderful time with the students. I was chosen as one of the top ten teachers on the campus coming out of the chute!

I just had a marvelous time. A colleague by the name of Paul Hersey was chairman of the Management Department. He wasn't very friendly to me initially because the Dean had led me to his department, but I heard he was a great teacher.

He taught Organizational Behavior and Leadership. So I said, "Can I sit in on your course next semester?"

"Nobody audits my courses," he said. "If you want to take it for credit, you're welcome."

I couldn't believe it. I had a doctoral degree and he wanted me to take his course for credit—so I signed up.

The registrar didn't know what to do with me because I already had a doctorate, but I wrote the papers and took the course, and it was great.

In June 1967, Hersey came into my office and said, "Ken, I've been teaching in this field for ten years. I think I'm better than anybody, but I can't write. I'm a nervous wreck, and I'd love to write a textbook with somebody. Would you write one with me?"

I said, "We ought to be a great team. You can't write and I'm not supposed to be able to, so let's do it!"

Thus began this great career of writing and teaching. We wrote a textbook called *Management of Organizational Behavior: Utilizing Human Resources*. It came out in its eighth edition October 3, 2000, and the ninth edition was published September 3, 2007. It has sold more than any other textbook in that area over the years. It's been over forty years since that book first came out.

I quit my administrative job, became a professor, and ended up working my way up the ranks. I got a sabbatical leave and went to California for one year twenty-five years ago. I ended up meeting Spencer Johnson at a cocktail party. He wrote children's books—a wonderful series called *Value Tales® for Kids*. He also wrote *The Value of Courage: The Story of Jackie Robinson* and *The Value of Believing In Yourself: The Story of Louis Pasteur*.

My wife, Margie, met him first and said, "You guys ought to write a children's book for managers because they won't read anything else." That was my introduction to Spencer. So, *The One Minute Manager* was really a kid's book for big people. That is a long way from saying that my career was well planned.

Wright

Ken, what and/or who were your early influences in the areas of business, leadership, and success? In other words, who shaped you in your early years?

Blanchard

My father had a great impact on me. He was retired as an admiral in the Navy and had a wonderful philosophy. I remember when I was elected as president of the seventh grade, and I came home all pumped up. My father said, "Son, it's great that you're the president of the seventh grade, but now that you have that leadership position, don't ever use it." He said, "Great leaders are followed because people respect them and like them, not because they have power." That was a wonderful lesson for me early on. He was just a great model for me. I got a lot from him.

Then I had this wonderful opportunity in the mid-1980s to write a book with

Norman Vincent Peale. He wrote *The Power of Positive Thinking*. I met him when he was eighty-six years old; we were asked to write a book on ethics together, *The Power of Ethical Management: Integrity Pays, You Don't Have to*

Cheat to Win. It didn't matter what we were writing together; I learned so much from him. He just built from the positive things I learned from my mother.

My mother said that when I was born I laughed before I cried, I danced before I walked, and I smiled before I frowned. So that, as well as Norman Vincent Peale, really impacted me as I focused on what I could do to train leaders. How do you make them positive? How do you make them realize that it's not about them, it's about who they are serving? It's not about their position—it's about what they can do to help other people win.

So, I'd say my mother and father, then Norman Vincent Peale. All had a tremendous impact on me.

Wright

I can imagine. I read a summary of your undergraduate and graduate degrees. I assumed you studied Business Administration, marketing management, and related courses. Instead, at Cornell you studied Government and Philosophy. You received your master's from Colgate in Sociology and Counseling and your PhD from Cornell in Educational Administration and Leadership. Why did you choose this course of study? How has it affected your writing and consulting?

Blanchard

Well, again, it wasn't really well planned out. I originally went to Colgate to get a master's degree in Education because I was going to be a Dean of Students over men. I had been a Government major, and I was a Government major because it was the best department at Cornell in the Liberal Arts School. It was exciting. We would study what the people were doing at the league of governments. And then, the Philosophy Department was great. I just loved the philosophical arguments. I wasn't a great student in terms of getting grades, but I'm a total learner. I would sit there and listen, and I would really soak it in.

When I went over to Colgate and got into the education courses, they were awful. They were boring. The second week, I was sitting at the bar at the Colgate Inn saying, "I can't believe I've been here two years for this." This is just the way the Lord works: Sitting next to me in the bar was a young sociology professor who had just gotten his PhD at Illinois. He was staying at the Inn. I was moaning and groaning about what I was doing, and he said, "Why don't you come and major with me in sociology? It's really exciting."

"I can do that?" I asked.

He said, "Yes."

I knew they would probably let me do whatever I wanted the first week.

Suddenly, I switched out of Education and went with Warren Ramshaw. He had a tremendous impact on me. He retired some years ago as the leading professor at Colgate in the Arts and Sciences, and got me interested in leadership and organizations. That's why I got a master's in Sociology.

The reason I went into educational administration and leadership? It was a doctoral program I could get into because I knew the guy heading up the program. He said, "The greatest thing about Cornell is that you will be in the School of Education. It's not very big, so you don't have to take many education courses, and you can take stuff all over the place."

There was a marvelous man by the name of Don McCarty who eventually became the Dean of the School of Education, Wisconsin. He had an impact on my life; but I was always just searching around.

My mission statement is: to be a loving teacher and example of simple truths that help myself and others to awaken the presence of God in our lives. The reason I mention "God" is that I believe the biggest addiction in the world is the human ego; but I'm really into simple truth. I used to tell people I was trying to get the B.S. out of the behavioral sciences.

Wright

I can't help but think, when you mentioned your father, that he just bottom-lined it for you about leadership.

Blanchard

Yes.

Wright

A man named Paul Myers, in Texas, years and years ago when I went to a conference down there, said, "David, if you think you're a leader and you look around, and no one is following you, you're just out for a walk."

Blanchard

Well, you'd get a kick out of this—I'm just reaching over to pick up a picture of Paul Myers on my desk. He's a good friend, and he's a part of our Center for FaithWalk Leadership where we're trying to challenge and equip people to lead like Jesus. It's non-profit. I tell people I'm not an evangelist because we've got enough trouble with the Christians we have. We don't need any more new ones. But, this is a picture of Paul on top of a mountain. Then there's another picture below that of him under the sea with stingrays. It says, "Attitude is everything. Whether you're on the top of the mountain or the bottom of the sea, true happiness is achieved by accepting God's promises, and by having a biblically positive frame of mind. Your attitude is everything." Isn't that something?

Wright

He's a fine, fine man. He helped me tremendously. In keeping with the theme of our book, *Discover Your Inner Strength,* I wanted to get a sense from you about your own success journey. Many people know you best from *The One Minute Manager* books you coauthored with Spencer Johnson. Would you consider these books as a high water mark for you or have you defined success for yourself in different terms?

Blanchard

Well, you know, *The One Minute Manager* was an absurdly successful book so quickly that I found I couldn't take credit for it. That was when I really got on my own spiritual journey and started to try to find out what the real meaning of life and success was.

That's been a wonderful journey for me because I think, David, the problem with most people is they think their self-worth is a function of their performance plus the opinion of others. The minute you think that is what your self-worth is, every day your self-worth is up for grabs because your performance is going to fluctuate on a day-to-day basis. People are fickle. Their opinions are going to go up and down. You need to ground your self-worth in the unconditional love that God has ready for us, and that really grew out of the unbelievable success of *The One Minute Manager*.

When I started to realize where all that came from, that's how I got involved in this ministry that I mentioned. Paul Myers is a part of it. As I started to read the Bible, I realized that everything I've ever written about, or taught, Jesus did. You know, He did it with the twelve incompetent guys He "hired." The only guy with much education was Judas, and he was His only turnover problem.

Wright

Right.

Blanchard

This is a really interesting thing. What I see in people is not only do they think their self-worth is a function of their performance plus the opinion of others, but they measure their success on the amount of accumulation of wealth, on recognition, power, and status. I think those are nice success items. There's nothing wrong with those, as long as you don't define your life by that.

What I think you need to focus on rather than success is what Bob Buford, in his book *Halftime,* calls "significance"—moving from success to significance. I think the opposite of accumulation of wealth is generosity.

I wrote a book called *The Generosity Factor* with Truett Cathy, who is the founder of Chick-fil-A. He is one of the most generous men I've ever met in my life. I thought we needed to have a model of generosity. It's not only your *treasure*, but it's your *time* and *talent*. Truett and I added *touch* as a fourth one.

The opposite of recognition is service. I think you become an adult when you realize you're here to serve rather than to be served.

Finally, the opposite of power and status is loving relationships. Take Mother Teresa as an example—she couldn't have cared less about recognition, power, and status because she was focused on generosity, service, and loving relationships; but she got all of that earthly stuff. If you focus on the earthly, such as money, recognition, and power, you're never going to get to significance. But if you focus on significance, you'll be amazed at how much success can come your way.

Wright

I spoke with Truett Cathy recently and was impressed by what a down-to-earth, good man he seems to be. When you start talking about him closing his restaurants on Sunday, all of my friends—when they found out I had talked to him—said, "Boy, he must be a great Christian man, but he's rich." I told them, "Well, to put his faith into perspective, by closing on Sunday it costs him $500 million a year." He lives his faith, doesn't he?

Blanchard

Absolutely, but he still outsells everybody else.

Wright

That's right.

Blanchard

According to their January 25, 2007, press release, Chick-fil-A was the nation's second-largest quick-service chicken restaurant chain in sales at that time. Its business performance marks the thirty-ninth consecutive year the chain has enjoyed a system-wide sales gain—a streak the company has sustained since opening its first chain restaurant in 1967.

Wright

The simplest market scheme, I told him, tripped me up. I walked by his first
Chick-fil-A I had ever seen, and some girl came out with chicken stuck on toothpicks and handed me one; I just grabbed it and ate it; it's history from there on.

Blanchard

Yes, I think so. It's really special. It is so important that people understand generosity, service, and loving relationships because too many people are running around like a bunch of peacocks. You even see pastors who measure their success by how many are in their congregation; authors by how many books they have sold; businesspeople by what their profit margin is—how good sales are. The reality is, that's all well and good, but I think what you need to focus on is the other. I think if business did that more and we got Wall Street off our backs with all the short-term evaluation, we'd be a lot better off.

Wright

Absolutely. There seems to be a clear theme that winds through many of your books that has to do with success in business and organizations—how people are treated by management and how they feel about their value to a company. Is this an accurate observation? If so, can you elaborate on it?

Blanchard

Yes, it's a very accurate observation. See, I think the profit is the applause you get for taking care of your customers and creating a motivating environment for your people. Very often people think that business is only about the bottom line. But no, that happens to be the result of creating raving fan customers, which I've described with Sheldon Bowles in our book, *Raving Fans*. Customers want to brag about you, if you create an environment where people can be gung-ho and committed. You've got to take care of your customers and your people, and then your cash register is going to go ka-ching, and you can make some big bucks.

Wright

I noticed that your professional title with the Ken Blanchard Companies is somewhat unique—"Chairman and Chief Spiritual Officer." What does your title mean to you personally and to your company? How does it affect the books you choose to write?

Blanchard

I remember having lunch with Max DuPree one time. The legendary Chairman of Herman Miller, Max wrote a wonderful book called *Leadership Is an Art*.

"What's your job?" I asked him.

He said, "I basically work in the vision area."

"Well, what do you do?" I asked.

"I'm like a third-grade teacher," he replied. "I say our vision and values over, and over, and over again until people get it right, right, right."

I decided from that, I was going to become the Chief Spiritual Officer, which means I would be working in the vision, values, and energy part of our business. I ended up leaving a morning message every day for everybody in our company. We have twenty-eight international offices around the world. I leave a voice mail every morning, and I do three things on that as Chief Spiritual Officer: One, people tell me who we need to pray for. Two, people tell me who we need to praise—our unsung heroes and people like that. And then three, I leave an inspirational morning message. I really am the cheerleader—the Energizer Bunny—in our company. I'm the reminder of why we're here and what we're trying to do.

We think that our business in the Ken Blanchard Companies is to help people lead at a higher level, and to help individuals and organizations. Our mission statement is to unleash the power and potential of people and organizations for the common good. So if we are going to do that, we've really got to believe in that.

I'm working on getting more Chief Spiritual Officers around the country. I think it's a great title and we should get more of them.

Wright

So those people for whom you pray, where do you get the names?

Blanchard

The people in the company tell me who needs help, whether it's a spouse who is sick or kids who are sick or if they are worried about something. We've got over five years of data about the power of prayer, which is pretty important.

One morning, my inspirational message was about my wife and five members of our company who walked sixty miles one weekend—twenty miles a day for three days—to raise money for breast cancer research.

It was amazing. I went down and waved them all in as they came. They had a ceremony; they had raised $7.6 million. There were over three thousand people walking. A lot of the walkers were dressed in pink—they were cancer victors— people who had overcome it. There were even men walking with pictures of their wives who had died from breast cancer. I thought it was incredible.

There wasn't one mention about it in the major San Diego papers. I said, "Isn't that just something." We have to be an island of positive influence because all you see in the paper today is about celebrities and their bad behavior. Here you have all these thousands of people out there walking and trying to make a difference, and nobody thinks it's news.

So every morning I pump people up about what life's about, about what's going on. That's what my Chief Spiritual Officer job is about.

Wright

I had the pleasure of reading one of your releases, *The Leadership Pill*.

Blanchard

Yes.

Wright

I must admit that my first thought was how short the book was. I wondered if I was going to get my money's worth, which by the way, I most certainly did. Many of your books are brief and based on a fictitious story. Most business books in the market today are hundreds of pages in length and are read almost like a textbook.

Will you talk a little bit about why you write these short books, and about the premise of *The Leadership Pill?*

Blanchard

I really developed my relationship with Spencer Johnson when we wrote *The One Minute Manager*. As you know, he wrote, *Who Moved My Cheese*, which was a phenomenal success. He wrote children's books and is quite a storyteller. Jesus taught by parables, which were short stories.

My favorite books are *Jonathan Livingston Seagull* and *The Little Prince*. Og Mandino, author of seventeen books, was the greatest of them all.

I started writing parables because people can get into the story and learn the contents of the story, and they don't bring their judgmental hats into reading. You write a regular book and they'll say, "Well, where did you get the research?" They get into that judgmental side. Our books get them emotionally involved and they learn.

The Leadership Pill is a fun story about a pharmaceutical company that thinks they have discovered the secret to leadership, and they can put the ingredients in a pill. When they announce it, the country goes crazy because everybody knows we need more effective leaders. When they release it, it outsells Viagra.

The founders of the company start selling off stock and they call them Pillionaires. But along comes this guy who calls himself "the effective manager," and he challenges them to a no-pill challenge. If they identify two non-performing groups, he'll take on one and let somebody on the pill take another one, and he guarantees he will outperform that person by the end of the year. They agree, but of course they give him a drug test every week to make sure he's not sneaking pills on the side.

I wrote the book with Marc Muchnick, who is a young guy in his early thirties.

We did a major study of what this interesting "Y" generation—the young people of today—want from leaders, and this is a secret blend that this effective manager uses. When you think about it, David, it is really powerful in terms of what people want from a leader.

Number one, they want integrity. A lot of people have talked about that in the past, but these young people will walk if they see people say one thing and do another. A lot of us walk to the bathroom and out into the halls to talk about it. But these people will quit. They don't want somebody to say something and not do it.

The second thing they want is a partnership relationship. They hate superior/subordinate. I mean, what awful terms those are. You know, the "head" of the department and the hired "hands"—you don't even give them a head. "What do I do? I'm in supervision. I see things a lot clearer than these stupid idiots." They want to be treated as partners; if they can get a financial partnership, great. If they can't, they really want a minimum of a psychological partnership where they can bring their brains to work and make decisions.

Then finally, they want affirmation. They not only want to be caught doing things right, but they want to be affirmed for who they are. They want to be known as individual people, not as numbers.

So those are the three ingredients that this effective manager uses. They are wonderful values when you think about them.

Rank-order values for any organization is number one, integrity. In our company we call it ethics. It is our number one value. The number two value is partnership. In our company we call it relationships. Number three is affirmation—being affirmed as a human being. I think that ties into relationships, too. They are wonderful values that can drive behavior in a great way.

Wright

I believe most people in today's business culture would agree that success in business has everything to do with successful leadership. In *The Leadership Pill*, you present a simple but profound premise; that leadership is not something you do to people; it's something you do *with* them. At face value, that seems incredibly obvious. But you must have found in your research and observations that leaders in today's culture do not get this. Would you speak to that issue?

Blanchard

Yes. I think what often happens in this is the human ego. There are too many leaders out there who are self-serving. They're not leaders who have service in mind. They think the sheep are there for the benefit of the shepherd. All the power, money, fame, and recognition move up the hierarchy. They forget that the real action in business is not up the hierarchy—it's in the one-to-one, moment-to-moment interactions that your frontline people have with your customers. It's how the phone is answered. It's how problems are dealt with and those kinds of things. If you don't think that you're doing leadership *with* them—rather, you're doing it *to* them—after a while they won't take care of your customers.

I was at a store once (not Nordstrom's, where I normally would go) and I thought of something I had to share with my wife, Margie. I asked the guy behind the counter in Men's Wear, "May I use your phone?"

He said, "No!"

"You're kidding me," I said. "I can always use the phone at Nordstrom's."

"Look, buddy," he said, "they won't let *me* use the phone here. Why should I let you use the phone?"

That is an example of leadership that's done *to* employees, not *with* them. People want a partnership. People want to be involved in a way that really makes a difference.

Wright

Dr. Blanchard, the time has flown by and there are so many more questions I'd like to ask you. In closing, would you mind sharing with our readers some thoughts on success? If you were mentoring a small group of men and women, and one of their central goals was to become successful, what kind of advice would you give them?

Blanchard

Well, I would first of all say, "What are you focused on?" If you are focused on success as being, as I said earlier, accumulation of money, recognition, power, or status, I think you've got the wrong target. What you need to really be focused on is how you can be generous in the use of your time and your talent and your treasure and touch. How can you serve people rather than be served? How can you develop caring, loving relationships with people? My sense is if you will focus on those things, success in the traditional sense will come to you. But if you go out and say, "Man, I'm going to make a fortune, and I'm going to do this," and have that kind of attitude, you might get some of those numbers. I think you become an adult, however, when you realize you are here to give rather than to get. You're here to serve, not to be served. I would just say to people, "Life is such a very special occasion. Don't miss it by aiming at a target that bypasses other people, because we're really here to serve each other."

Wright

Well, what an enlightening conversation, Dr. Blanchard. I really want you to know how much I appreciate all the time you've taken with me for this interview. I know that our readers will learn from this, and I really appreciate your being with us today.

Blanchard

Well, thank you so much, David. I really enjoyed my time with you. You've asked some great questions that made me think, and I hope my answers are helpful to other people because as I say, life is a special occasion.

Wright

Today we have been talking with Dr. Ken Blanchard. He is coauthor of the phenomenal best-selling book, *The One Minute Manager*. The fact that he's the Chief Spiritual Officer of his company should make us all think about how we are leading our companies and leading our families and leading anything, whether it is in church or civic organizations. I know I will.

Thank you so much, Dr. Blanchard, for being with us today.

Blanchard

Good to be with you, David.

Few people have created more of a positive impact on the day-to-day management of people and companies than Dr. Kenneth Blanchard, who is known around the world simply as "Ken."

When Ken speaks, he speaks from the heart with warmth and humor. His unique gift is to speak to an audience and communicate with each individual as if they were alone and talking one-on-one. He is a polished storyteller with a knack for making the seemingly complex easy to understand.

Ken has been a guest on a number of national television programs, including *Good Morning America* and *The Today Show*. He has been featured in *Time*, *People*, *U.S. News & World Report*, and a host of other popular publications.

He earned his bachelor's degree in Government and Philosophy from Cornell University, his master's degree in Sociology and Counseling from Colgate University, and his PhD in Educational Administration and Leadership from Cornell University.

Dr. Ken Blanchard
The Ken Blanchard Companies
125 State Place
Escondido, California 92029
800.728.6000
Fax: 760.489.8407
www.kenblanchard.com

CHAPTER THREE
A Values-Based Approach

An Interview With...
Dr. Stephen Covey

David Wright (Wright)

We're talking today with Dr. Stephen R. Covey, cofounder and vice-chairman of Franklin Covey Company, the largest management company and leadership development organization in the world. Dr. Covey is perhaps best known as author of *The 7 Habits of Highly Effective People,* which is ranked as a number one best-seller by the *New York Times,* having sold more than fourteen million copies in thirty-eight languages throughout the world. Dr. Covey is an internationally respected leadership authority, family expert, teacher, and organizational consultant. He has made teaching principle-centered living and principle-centered leadership his life's work. Dr. Covey is the recipient of the Thomas More College Medallion for Continuing Service to

Humanity and has been awarded four honorary doctorate degrees. Other awards given Dr. Covey include the Sikh's 1989 International Man of Peace award, the 1994 International Entrepreneur of the Year award, *Inc.* magazine's Services Entrepreneur of the Year award, and in 1996 the

National Entrepreneur of the Year Lifetime Achievement award for Entrepreneurial leadership. He has also been recognized as one of *Time* magazine's twenty-five most influential Americans and one of *Sales and Marketing Management's* top twenty-five power brokers. As the father of nine and grandfather of forty-four, Dr. Covey received the 2003 National Fatherhood Award, which he says is the most meaningful award he has ever received. Dr. Covey earned his undergraduate degree from the University of Utah, his MBA from Harvard, and completed his doctorate at Brigham Young University. While at Brigham Young he served as assistant to the President and was also a professor of Business Management and Organizational Behavior.

Dr. Covey, welcome to *Discover Your Inner Strength*.

Dr. Stephen Covey (Covey)
Thank you.

Wright
Dr. Covey, most companies make decisions and filter them down through their organization. You, however, state that no company can succeed until individuals within it succeed. Are the goals of the company the result of the combined goals of the individuals?

Covey
Absolutely—if people aren't on the same page, they're going to be pulling in different directions. To teach this concept, I frequently ask large audiences to close their eyes and point north, and then to keep pointing and open their eyes. They find themselves pointing all over the place. I say to them, "Tomorrow morning if you want a similar experience, ask the first ten people you meet in your organization what the purpose of your organization is and you'll find it's a very similar experience.

They'll point all over the place." When people have a different sense of purpose and values, every decision that is made from then on is governed by those. There's no question that this is one of the fundamental causes of misalignment, low trust, interpersonal conflict, interdepartmental rivalry, people operating on personal agendas, and so forth.

Wright
Is that primarily a result of an inability to communicate from the top?

Covey

That's one aspect, but I think it's more fundamental. There's an inability to involve people—an unwillingness. Leaders may communicate what their mission and their strategy is, but that doesn't mean there's any emotional connection to it. Mission statements that are rushed and then announced are soon forgotten. They become nothing more than just a bunch of platitudes on the wall that mean essentially nothing and even create a source of cynicism and a sense of hypocrisy inside the culture of an organization.

Wright

How do companies ensure survival and prosperity in these tumultuous times of technological advances, mergers, downsizing, and change?

Covey

I think that it takes a lot of high trust in a culture that has something that doesn't change—principles—at its core. There are principles that people agree upon that are valued. It gives a sense of stability. Then you have the power to adapt and be flexible when you experience these kinds of disruptive new economic models or technologies that come in and sideswipe you. You don't know how to handle them unless you have something you can depend upon.

If people have not agreed to a common set of principles that guide them and a common purpose, then they get their security from the outside and they tend to freeze the structure, systems, and processes inside and they cease becoming adaptable. They don't change with the changing realities of the new marketplace out there and gradually they become obsolete.

Wright

I was interested in one portion of your book, *The 7 Habits of Highly Effective People,* where you talk about behaviors. How does an individual go about the process of replacing ineffective behaviors with effective ones?

Covey

I think that for most people it usually requires a crisis that humbles them to become aware of their ineffective behaviors. If there's not a crisis the tendency is to perpetuate those behaviors and not change.

You don't have to wait until the marketplace creates the crisis for you. Have everyone accountable on a 360-degree basis to everyone else they interact with— with feedback either formal or informal—where they are getting data as to what's happening. They will then start to realize that the consequences of their ineffective behavior require them to be humble enough to look at that behavior and to adopt new, more effective ways of doing things.

Sometimes people can be stirred up to this if you just appeal to their conscience—to their inward sense of what is right and wrong. A lot of people sometimes know inwardly they're doing wrong, but the culture doesn't necessarily discourage them from continuing that. They either need feedback from people or they need feedback from the marketplace or they need feedback from their conscience. Then they can begin to develop a step-by-step process of replacing old habits with new, better habits.

Wright

It's almost like saying, "Let's make all the mistakes in the laboratory before we put this thing in the air."

Covey

Right; and I also think what is necessary is a paradigm shift, which is analogous to having a correct map, say of a city or of a country. If people have an inaccurate paradigm of life, of other people, and of themselves it really doesn't make much difference what their behavior or habits or attitudes are. What they need is a correct paradigm—a correct map—that describes what's going on.

For instance, in the Middle Ages they used to heal people through bloodletting. It wasn't until Samuel Weiss and Pasteur and other empirical scientists discovered the germ theory that they realized for the first time they weren't dealing with the real issue. They realized why women preferred to use midwives who washed rather than doctors who didn't wash. They gradually got a new paradigm. Once you've got a new paradigm then your behavior and your attitude flow directly from it. If you have a bad paradigm or a bad map, let's say of a city, there's no way, no matter what your behavior or your habits or your attitudes are—how positive they are—you'll never be able to find the location you're looking for. This is why I believe that to change paradigms is far more fundamental than to work on attitude and behavior.

Wright

One of your seven habits of highly effective people is to "begin with the end in mind." If circumstances change and hardships or miscalculations occur, how does one view the end with clarity?

Covey

Many people think to begin with the end in mind means that you have some fixed definition of a goal that's accomplished and if changes come about you're not going to adapt to them. Instead, the "end in mind" you begin with is that you are going to create a flexible culture of high trust so that no matter what comes along you are going to do whatever it takes to accommodate that new change or that new reality and maintain a culture of high performance and high trust. You're talking more in terms of values and overall purposes that don't change, rather than specific strategies or programs that will have to change to accommodate the changing realities in the marketplace.

Wright

In this time of mistrust among people, corporations, and nations, for that matter, how do we create high levels of trust?

Covey

That's a great question and it's complicated because there are so many elements that go into the creating of a culture of trust. Obviously the most fundamental one is just to have trustworthy people. But that is not sufficient because what if the organization itself is misaligned?

For instance, what if you say you value cooperation but you really reward people for internal competition? Then you have a systemic or a structure problem that creates low trust inside the culture even though the people themselves are trustworthy. This is one of the insights of Edward Demming and the work he did.

That's why he said that most problems are not personal—they're systemic. They're common caused. That's why you have to work on structure, systems, and processes to make sure that they institutionalize principle-centered values. Otherwise you could have good people with bad systems and you'll get bad results.

When it comes to developing interpersonal trust between people, it is made up of many, many elements such as taking the time to listen to other people, to understand them, and to see what is important to them. What we think is important to another may only be important to us, not to another. It takes empathy. You have to make and keep promises to them. You have to treat people with kindness and courtesy. You have to be completely honest and open. You have to live up to your commitments. You can't betray people behind their back. You can't badmouth them behind their back and sweet-talk

41

them to their face. That will send out vibes of hypocrisy and it will be detected.

You have to learn to apologize when you make mistakes, to admit mistakes, and to also get feedback going in every direction as much as possible. It doesn't necessarily require formal forums—it requires trust between people who will be

open with each other and give each other feedback.

Wright

My mother told me to do a lot of what you're saying now, but it seems that when I got in business I simply forgot.

Covey

Sometimes we forget, but sometimes culture doesn't nurture it. That's why I say unless you work with the institutionalizing—that means formalizing into structure, systems, and processing the values—you will not have a nurturing culture. You have to constantly work on that.

This is one of the big mistakes organizations make. They think trust is simply a function of being honest. That's only one small aspect. It's an important aspect, obviously, but there are so many other elements that go into the creation of a hightrust culture.

Wright

"Seek first to understand then to be understood" is another of your seven habits.

Do you find that people try to communicate without really understanding what other people want?

Covey

Absolutely. The tendency is to project out of our own autobiography—our own life, our own value system—onto other people, thinking we know what they want. So we don't really listen to them. We pretend to listen, but we really don't listen from within their frame of reference. We listen from within our own frame of reference and we're really preparing our reply rather than seeking to understand. This is a very common thing. In fact, very few people have had any training in seriously listening.

They're trained in how to read, write, and speak, but not to listen.

Reading, writing, speaking, and listening are the four modes of communication and they represent about two-thirds to three-fourths of our waking hours. About half of that time is spent listening, but it's the one skill people have not been trained in.

People have had all this training in the other forms of communication. In a large audience of 1,000 people you wouldn't have more than twenty people who have had more than two weeks of training in listening. Listening is more than a skill or technique; you must listen within another's frame of reference. It takes tremendous courage to listen because you're at risk when you listen. You don't know what's going to happen; you're vulnerable.

Wright

Sales gurus always tell me that the number one skill in selling is listening.

Covey

Yes—listening from within the customer's frame of reference. That is so true.

You can see that it takes some security to do that because you don't know what's going to happen.

Wright

With this book we're trying to encourage people to be better, to live better, and be more fulfilled by listening to the examples of our guest authors. Is there anything or anyone in your life that has made a difference for you and helped you to become a better person?

Covey

I think the most influential people in my life have been my parents. I think that what they modeled was not to make comparisons and harbor jealousy or to seek recognition. They were humble people.

I remember one time when my mother and I were going up in an elevator and the most prominent person in the state was also in the elevator. She knew him, but she spent her time talking to the elevator operator. I was just a little kid and I was so awed by the famous person. I said to her, "Why didn't you talk to the important person?" She said, "I was. I had never met him."

My parents were really humble, modest people who were focused on service and other people rather than on themselves. I think they were very inspiring models to me.

Wright

In almost every research paper I've ever read, those who write about people who have influenced their lives include three teachers in their top-five picks. My seventh grade English teacher was the greatest teacher I ever had and she influenced me to no end.

Covey

Would it be correct to say that she saw in you probably some qualities of greatness you didn't even see in yourself?

Wright

Absolutely.

Covey

That's been my general experience—the key aspect of a mentor or a teacher is someone who sees in you potential that you don't even see in yourself. Those teachers/mentors treat you accordingly and eventually you come to see it in yourself.

That's my definition of leadership or influence—communicating people's worth and potential so clearly that they are inspired to see it in themselves.

Wright

Most of my teachers treated me as a student, but she treated me with much more respect than that. As a matter of fact, she called me Mr. Wright, and I was in the seventh grade at the time. I'd never been addressed by anything but a nickname. I stood a little taller; she just made a tremendous difference.

Do you think there are other characteristics that mentors seem to have in common?

Covey

I think they are first of all good examples in their own personal lives. Their personal lives and their family lives are not all messed up—they come from a base of good character. They also are usually very confident and they take the time to do what your teacher did to you—to treat you with uncommon respect and courtesy.

They also, I think, explicitly teach principles rather than practices so that rules don't take the place of human judgment. You gradually come to have faith in your own judgment in making decisions because of the affirmation of such a mentor. Good mentors care about you—you can feel the sincerity of their caring. It's like the expression, "I don't care how much you know until I know how much you care."

Wright

Most people are fascinated with the new television shows about being a survivor.

What has been the greatest comeback that you've made from adversity in your career or your life?

Covey

When I was in grade school I experienced a disease in my legs. It caused me to use crutches for a while. I tried to get off them fast and get back. The disease wasn't corrected yet so I went back on crutches for another year. The disease went to the other leg and I went on for another year. It essentially took me out of my favorite thing—athletics—and it took me more into being a student. So that was a life defining experience, which at the time seemed very negative, but has proven to be the basis on which I've focused my life— being more of a learner.

Wright

Principle-centered learning is basically what you do that's different from anybody I've read or listened to.

Covey

The concept is embodied in the Far Eastern expression, "Give a man a fish, you feed him for the day; teach him how to fish, you feed him for a lifetime." When you teach principles that are universal and timeless, they don't belong to just any one person's religion or to a particular culture or geography. They seem to be timeless and universal like the ones we've been talking about here: trustworthiness, honesty, caring, service, growth, and development. These are universal principles. If you focus on these things, then little by little people become independent of you and then they start to believe in themselves and their own judgment becomes better. You don't need as many rules. You don't need as much bureaucracy and as many controls and you can empower people.

The problem in most business operations today—and not just business but nonbusiness— is that they're using the industrial model in an information age. Arnold

45

Toynbee, the great historian, said, "You can pretty well summarize all of history in four words: nothing fails like success." The industrial model was based on the asset of the machine. The information model is based on the asset of the person—the knowledge worker. It's an altogether different model. But the machine model was the main asset of the twentieth century. It enabled productivity to increase fifty times. The new asset is intellectual and social capital—the qualities of people and the quality of the relationship they have with each other. Like Toynbee said, "Nothing fails like success." The industrial model does not work in an information age. It requires a focus on the new wealth, not capital and material things.

A good illustration that demonstrates how much we were into the industrial model, and still are, is to notice where people are on the balance sheet. They're not found there. Machines are found there. Machines become investments. People are on the profit-and-loss statement and people are expenses. Think of that—if that isn't bloodletting.

Wright

It sure is.

When you consider the choices you've made down through the years, has faith played an important role in your life?

Covey

It has played an extremely important role. I believe deeply that we should put principles at the center of our lives, but I believe that God is the source of those principles. I did not invent them. I get credit sometimes for some of the Seven Habits material and some of the other things I've done, but it's really all based on principles that have been given by God to all of His children from the beginning of time. You'll find that you can teach these same principles from the sacred texts and the wisdom literature of almost any tradition. I think the ultimate source of that is God and that is one thing you can absolutely depend upon—"in God we trust."

Wright

If you could have a platform and tell our audience something you feel would help them or encourage them, what would you say?

Covey

I think I would say to put God at the center of your life and then prioritize your family. No one on their deathbed ever wished they had spent more time at the office.

Wright

That's right. We have come down to the end of our program and I know you're a busy person. I could talk with you all day, Dr. Covey.

Covey

It's good to talk with you as well and to be a part of this program. It looks like an excellent one that you've got going on here.

Wright

Thank you.

We have been talking today with Dr. Stephen R. Covey, cofounder and vice chairman of Franklin Covey Company. He's also the author of *The 7 Habits of Highly Effective People,* which has been ranked as a number one bestseller by the *New York Times*, selling more than fourteen million copies in thirty-eight languages.

Dr. Covey, thank you so much for being with us today.

Covey

Thank you for the honor of participating.

ABOUT THE AUTHOR

Stephen R. Covey was recognized in 1996 as one of *Time* magazine's twenty-five most influential Americans and one of *Sales and Marketing Management's* top twenty-five power brokers. Dr. Covey is the author of several acclaimed books, including the international bestseller, *The 7 Habits of Highly Effective People*, named the number one Most Influential Business Book of the Twentieth Century, and other best sellers that include *First Things First*, *Principle-Centered Leadership,* (with sales exceeding one million) and *The 7 Habits of Highly Effective Families.*

Dr. Covey earned his undergraduate degree from the University of Utah, his MBA from Harvard, and completed his doctorate at Brigham Young University. While at

Brigham Young University, he served as assistant to the President and was also a professor of Business Management and Organizational Behavior. He received the

National Fatherhood Award in 2003, which, as the father of nine and grandfather of forty-four, he says is the most meaningful award he has ever received. Dr. Covey currently serves on the board of directors for the Points of Light Foundation. Based in Washington, D.C., the Foundation, through its partnership with the Volunteer Center National Network, engages and mobilizes millions of volunteers from all walks of life—businesses, nonprofits, faith-based organizations, low-income communities, families, youth, and older adults—to help solve serious social problems in thousands of communities.

Dr. Stephen R. Covey
www.stephencovey.com

Chapter Four
Using Strategy to Discover Your Inner Strength

An Interview With...
Brian Tracy

David Wright (Wright)

Many years ago, Brian Tracy started off on a lifelong search for the secrets of success in life and business. He studied, researched, traveled, worked, and taught for more than thirty years. In 1981, he began to share his discoveries in talks and seminars, and eventually in books, audios and video-based courses.

The greatest secret of success he learned is this: "There are no secrets of success." There are instead timeless truths and principles that have to be rediscovered, relearned, and practiced by each person. Brian's gift is synthesis—the ability to take large numbers of ideas from many sources and combine them into highly practical, enjoyable, and immediately usable forms that people can take and apply quickly to improve their life and work. Brian has brought together the best ideas, methods, and techniques from thousands of books, hundreds of courses, and experience working with individuals and organizations of every kind in the U.S., Canada, and worldwide.

Today, I have asked Brian to discuss his latest book, *Victory!: Applying the Military Principals of Strategy for Success in Business and Personal Life.* Brian Tracy, welcome to *Discover Your Inner Strength.*

Tracy

Thank you, David. It's a pleasure to be here.

Wright

Let's talk about your new book the *Victory!: Applying* the *Military Principals* of *Strategy* for *Success* in *Business* and *Personal Life.* (By the way it is refreshing to hear someone say something good about the successes of the military.) Why do you think the military is so successful?

Tracy

Well, the military is based on very serious thought. The American military is the most respected institution in America. Unless you're a left liberal limp-wristed pinko most people in America really respect the military because it keeps America free.

People who join the military give up most of their lives—twenty to thirty years—in sacrifice to be prepared to guard our freedoms. And if you ask around the world what it is that America stands for, it stands for individual freedom, liberty, democracy, freedom, and opportunity that is only secured in a challenging world—a dangerous world—by your military.

Now the other thing is that the people in our military are not perfect because there is no human institution made up of human beings that is perfect—there are no perfect people. The cost of mistakes in military terms is death; therefore, people in the military are extraordinarily serious about what they do. They are constantly looking for ways to do what they do better and better and better to reduce the likelihood of losing a single person.

We in America place extraordinary value on individual human life. That is why you will see millions of dollars spent to save a life, whether for an accident victim or Siamese twins from South America, because that's part of our culture. The military has that same culture.

I was just reading today about the RQ-1 "Predator" drone planes (Unmanned Aerial Vehicles—UAVs) that have been used in reconnaissance over the no-fly zones in Iraq. These planes fly back and forth constantly gathering information from the ground. They can also carry remote-controlled weapons. According to www.globalsecurity.org, the planes cost $4.5 million each and get shot down on a regular basis. However, the military is willing to invest hundreds of millions of dollars to develop these planes, and lose them to save the life of a pilot, because pilots are so precious—human life is precious. In the military everything is calculated right down to the tinniest detail because it's the smallest details that can cost lives. That is why the military is so successful—they are so meticulous about planning.

A salesperson can go out and make a call; if it doesn't work that's fine—he or she can make another sales call. Professional soldiers can go out on an operation and if it's not successful they're dead and maybe everybody in the squad is dead as well.

There is no margin for error in the military; that's why they do it so well. This is also why the military principals of strategy that I talk about in *Victory!* are so incredibly important because a person who really understands those principals and strategies sees how to do things vastly better with far lower probability of failure than the average person.

Wright

In the promotion on *Victory!* you affirm that it is very important to set clear attainable goals and objectives. Does that theme carry out through all of your presentations and all of your books?

Tracy

Yes. Over and over again the theme reiterates that you can't hit a target you can't see—you shouldn't get into your car unless you know where you are going. More people spend more time planning a picnic than they spend planning their careers.

I'll give you an example. A very successful woman who is in her fifties now wrote down a plan when she was attending university. Her plan was for the first ten years she would work for a Fortune 500 corporation, really learn the business, and learn how to function at high levels. For the second ten years of her career she talked about getting married and having children at the same time. For that second ten years she would also work for a medium sized company helping it grow and succeed.

For the third ten years (between the ages of forty and fifty), she would start her own company based on her knowledge of both businesses. She would then build that into a successful company. Her last ten years she would be chief executive officer of a major corporation and retire financially independent at the age of sixty. At age fiftyeight she would have hit every single target. People would say, "Boy, you sure are lucky." No, it wouldn't be luck. From the time she was seventeen she was absolutely crystal clear about what she was going to do with her career and what she was going to do with her life, and she hit all of her targets.

Wright

In a time where companies, both large and small, take a look at their competition and basically try to copy everything they do, it was really interesting to read in *Victory!* that you suggest taking vigorous offensive action to get the best results. What do you mean by "vigorous offensive action"?

Tracy

Well, see, that's another thing. When you come back to talking about probabilities—and this is really important—you see successful people try more things. And if you wanted to just end the interview right now and ask, "What piece of advice would you give to our listeners?" I would say, "Try more things." The reason I would say that is because if you try more things, the probability is that you will hit your target

For example, here's an analogy I use. Imagine that you go into a room and there is a dartboard against the far wall. Now imagine that you are drunk and you have never played darts before. The room is not very bright and you can barely see the bull's eye. You are standing along way from the board, but you have an endless supply of darts. You pick up the darts and you just keep throwing them at the target over there on the other of the room even though you are not a good dart thrower and you're not even well coordinated. If you kept throwing darts over and over again what would you eventually hit?

Wright

Pretty soon you would get a bull's eye.

Tracy

Yes, eventually you would hit a bull's eye. The odds are that as you keep throwing the darts even though you are not that well educated, even if you don't come from a wealthy family or you don't have a Harvard education, if you just keep throwing darts you will get a little better each time you throw. It's known as a "decybernetic self correction mechanism" in the brain—each time you try something, you get a little bit smarter at it. So over time, if you kept throwing, you must eventually hit a bull's eye.

In other words, you must eventually find the right way to do the things you need to do to become a millionaire. That's the secret of success. That's why people come here from a 190 countries with one idea in mind—"If I come here I can try anything I want; I can go anywhere, because there are no limitations. I have so much freedom; and if I keep doing this, then by God, I will eventually hit a bull's eye." And they do and everybody says, "Boy, you sure where lucky."

Now imagine another scenario: You are thoroughly trained at throwing darts— you have practiced, you have developed skills and expertise in your field, you are constantly upgrading your knowledge, and you practice all the time. Second you are completely prepared, you're thoroughly cold sober, fresh, fit, alert, with high energy.

Third, all of the room is very bright around the dartboard. This time how long would it take you to hit the bull's eye? The obvious answer is you will hit a bull's eye far faster than if you had all those negative conditions.

What I am I saying is, you can dramatically increase the speed at which you hit your bull's eye. The first person I described—drunk, unprepared, in a darkened room, and so on—may take twenty or twenty-five years. But if you are thoroughly prepared, constantly upgrading your skills; if you are very clear about your targets; if you have everything you need at hand and your target is clear, your chances of hitting

a bull's eye you could hit a bull's eye is five years rather than twenty. That's the difference in success in life.

Wright

In reading your books and watching your presentations on video, one of the common threads seen through your presentations is creativity. I was glad that in the promotional material of *Victory!* you state that you need to apply innovative solutions to overcome obstacles. The word "innovative" grabbed me. I guess you are really concerned with *how* people solve problems rather than just solving problems.

Tracy

Vigorous action means you will cover more ground. What I say to people, especially in business, is the more things you do the more experience you get. The more experience you get the smarter you get. The smarter you get the better results you get the better results you get. The better results you get the less time it takes you to get the same results. And it's such a simple thing. In my books *Create Your Own Future* and *Victory!* you will find there is one characteristic of all successful people—they are action oriented. They move fast, they move quickly, and they don't waste time. They're moving ahead, trying more things, but they are always in motion.

The faster you move the more energy you have. The faster you move the more in control you feel and the faster you are the more positive and the more motivated you are. We are talking about a direct relationship between vigorous action and success.

Wright

Well, the military certainly is a team "sport" and you talk about building peak performance teams for maximum results. My question is how do individuals in corporations build peak performance teams in this culture?

Tracy

One of the things we teach is the importance of selecting people carefully. Really successful companies spend an enormous amount of time at the front end on selection they look for people who are really, really good in terms of what they are looking for. They interview very carefully; they interview several people and they interview them several times. They do careful background checks. They are as careful in selecting people as a person might be in getting married. Again, in the military, before a person is promoted they go through a rigorous process. In large corporations, before a person is promoted his or her performance is very, very carefully evaluated to be sure they are the right people to be promoted at that time.

Wright

My favorite point in *Victory!* is when you say, "Amaze your competitors with surprise and speed." I have done that several times in business and it does work like a charm.

Tracy

Yes, it does. Again one of the things we teach over and over again that there is a direct relationship between speed and perceived value. When you do things fast for people they consider you to be better. They consider your products to be better and they consider your service to be better—they actually consider them to be of higher value. Therefore, if you do things really, really fast then you overcome an enormous amount of resistance. People wonder, "Is this a good decision? Is it worth the money? Am I going the right direction?" When you do things fast, you blast that out of their minds.

Wright

You talk about moving quickly to seize opportunities. I have found that to be difficult. When I ask people about opportunities, it's difficult to find out what they think an opportunity is. Many think opportunities are high-risk, although I've never found it that way myself. What do you mean by moving quickly to cease opportunity?

Tracy

There are many cases were a person has an idea and they think that's a good idea.

They think they should do something about it. They think, "I am going to do something about that but I really can't do it this week, so I will wait until after the month ends," and so on. By the time they do move on the opportunity it's to late— somebody's already seized it.

One of the military examples I use is the battle of Gettysburg. Now the battle of Gettysburg was considered the high-water mark of the Confederacy after the battle of Gettysburg the Confederacy won additional battles at Chattanooga and other places but they eventually lost the war. The high-water mark of Gettysburg was a little hill at one end of the battlefield called Little Round Top. As the battle began

Little Round Top was empty. Colonel Joshua Chamberlain of the Union Army saw that this could be the pivotal point of the battlefield. He went up there and looked at it and he immediately rushed troops to fortify the hill. Meanwhile, the Confederates also saw that Little Round Top could be key to the battle as well, so they too immediately rushed the hill. An enormous battle took place. It was really the essence of the battle of Gettysburg. The victor who took that height controlled the battlefield. Eventually the union troops, who were almost lost, controlled Little Round Top and won the battle. The Civil War was over in about a year and a half, but that was the turning point.

So what would have happened if Chamberlain had said, "Wait until after lunch and then I'll move some men up to Little Round Top"? The Confederate troops would have seized Little Round Top, controlled the battlefield, and would have won the battle of Gettysburg. It was just a matter of moving very, very fast. Forty years later it was determined that there were three days at the battle of Gettysburg that cost the battle for the Confederates. The general in charge of the troops on the Confederate right flank was General James Longstreet. Lee told him to move his army forward as quickly as possible the next day, but to use his own judgment. Longstreet didn't agree with Lee's plan so he kept his troop sitting there most of the next day. It is said that it was Longstreet's failure to move forward on the second day and seize Little Round Top that cost the Confederacy the battle and eventually the war. It was just this failure to move forward and forty years later, when Longstreet appeared at a reunion of Confederate veterans in 1901 or 1904, he was booed. The veterans felt his failure to move forward that fateful day cost them the war. If you read every single account of the battle of Gettysburg, Longstreet's failure to move forward and quickly seize the opportunity is always included.

Wright

In your book you tell your readers to get the ideas and information needed to succeed. Where can individuals get these ideas?

Tracy

Well we are living in an ocean of ideas. It's so easy. The very first thing you do is you pick a subject you want to major in and you go to someone who is good at it.

You ask what you should read in this field and you go down to the bookstore and you look at the books. Any book that is published in paperback obviously sold well in hardcover. Read the table of contents. Make sure the writer has experience in the area you in which you want to learn about. Buy the book and read it. People ask,

"How can I be sure it is the right book?" You can't be sure; stop trying to be sure.

When I go to the bookstore I buy three or four books and bring them home and read them. I may only find one chapter of a book that's helpful, but that chapter may save me a year of hard work.

The fact is that your life is precious. A book costs twenty of thirty dollars. How much is your life worth? How much do you earn per hour? A person who earns fifty thousand dollars a year earns twenty-five dollars an hour. A person who wants to earn a hundred thousand dollars a year earns fifty dollars an hour. Now, if a book cost you ten or twenty dollars but it can save you a year of hard work, then that's the cheapest thing you have bought in your whole life. And what if you bought fifty books and you paid twenty dollars apiece for them—a thousand dollars worth of books—and out of that you only got one idea that saved you a year of hard work?

You've got a fifty times payoff. So the rule is you cannot prepare too thoroughly.

Wright

In the last several months I have recommended your book, *Get Paid More and Promoted Faster* to more people. I have had a lot of friends in their fifties and sixties who have lost their jobs to layoffs all kinds of transfers of ownership. When I talked with you last, the current economy had a 65 percent jump in layoffs. In the last few months before I talked with you, every one of them reported that the book really did help them. They saw some things a little bit clearer; it was a great book.

How do you turn setbacks and difficulties to your advantage? I know what it means, but what's the process?

Tracy

You look into it you look into every setback and problem and find the seed of an equal or greater advantage or benefit. It's a basic rule. You find that all successful people look into their problems for lessons they can learn and for things they can turn to their advantage. In fact, one of the best attitudes you can possibly have is to say that you know every problem that is sent to you is sent to help you. So your job is just simply look into to it and ask, "What can help me in this situation?" And surprise, surprise! You will find something that can help you. You will find lessons you can learn; you will find something you can do more of, or less of; you can find something that will give you an insight that will set you in a different direction, and so on.

Wright

I am curious. I know you have written a lot in the past and you are a terrific writer. Your cassette programs are wonderful. What do you have planned for the next few years?

Tracy

Aside from speaking and consulting with non-profits, my goal is to produce four books a year on four different subjects, all of which have practical application to help people become more successful.

Wright

Well, I really want to thank you for your time here today on *Discover Your Inner Strength!* It's always fascinating to hear what you have to say. I know I have been a Brian Tracy fan for many, many years. I really appreciate your being with us today.

Tracy

Thank you. You have a wonderful day and I hope our listeners and readers will go out and get *Focal Point* and/or *Victory!* They are available at any bookstore or at Amazon.com. They are fabulous books, filled with good ideas that will save you years of hard work.

Wright

I have already figured out that those last two books are a better buy with Amazon.com, so you should go to your computer and buy these books as soon as possible. We have been talking today with Brian Tracy, whose life and career truly makes one of the best rags-to-riches stories. Brian didn't graduate from high school and his first job was washing dishes. He lost job after job— washing cars, pumping gas, stacking lumber, you name it. He was homeless and living in his car. Finally, he got into sales, then sales management. Later, he sold investments, developed real estate, imported and distributed Japanese automobiles, and got a master's degree in business administration. Ultimately, he became the COO of a $265 million dollar development company.

Brian, you are quite a person. Thank you so much for being with us today.

Tracy

You are very welcome, David. You have a great day!

One of the world's top success motivational speakers, Brian Tracy is the author of many books and audio tape seminars, including *The Psychology of Achievement*, *The Luck Factor*, *Breaking the Success Barrier*, *Thinking Big* and *Success Is a Journey*.

Brian Tracy
www.BrianTracy.com